I0494762

Service, Please! Extra Pickles,

Hold the Attitude

Plating Up Customer Service for All Professionals

Teressa Shivers-Mazzei

Teressa Shivers-Mazzei

ISBN: 151732825X
ISBN 13: 9781517328252
Library of Congress Control Number: 2015919257
LCCN Imprint Name: CreateSpace Independent
Publishing Platform, North Charleston, SC

To my family and friends. They never stop believing in me. Without them I wouldn't have learned many of life's lessons.

To my sister, Susan, who pushes me to be the very best I can be, you see things in me that I don't always see in myself and ignite a fire in me to share what knowledge and ideas I have with others. You inspire me.

To my daughter, Adeline, you make me a proud *matka* every single day. May you always remember that your attitude will reflect who you are.

To my mom, you are my rock, and because of you I have two feet planted firmly on the ground.

I've learned that people will forget what you said, people will forget what you did, but people will never forget how you made them feel.

—Maya Angelou

INTRODUCTION

Welcome to *Service, Please! Extra Pickles, Hold the Attitude*. Do you honestly know why you chose customer service as your life's work? Or maybe you haven't chosen it as your life's work but it's helping you transition in your career. Think about what customer service means to you while you venture on and read this book.

Don't be fooled by the title, because I am not just addressing food service. If you serve people in any capacity, pull up a seat to this discussion table. Have you ever had a spectacular customer-service experience? I have, and it's something I'll never forget. That exact experience is what makes you crave more. In my opinion, attitude plays a big role in the customer's experience. If we roll our sleeves up and get down to the basics of how to treat customers by focusing on our individual attitudes, there will be a lot of satisfied customers out there. The framework of this book is formatted to resemble a restaurant menu. Every course of the meal can stand on its own, but the entire experience is enhanced when you understand the connection between all its parts and bring them together as a whole. Your attitude in providing service for your customers will then reach an entirely new level, allowing you to provide an experience your customers will talk about for a long time to come.

Before proceeding, answer these questions:

- Why have you decided to choose or are you thinking about choosing customer service as your profession?

- What three things can you offer as a professional in this field?

- In what ways has customer service affected you as a customer? Give an example.

I have inserted "Crumbs" pages throughout this book so you can jot down your thoughts.

When I asked customer-service professionals all over the United States why they loved their jobs, the common response was simply, "I love people."

Teressa Shivers-Mazzei

CRUMBS

WHAT WOULD YOU DO?

It's 10:15 p.m., give or take a couple of minutes. You have been slammed all day on your shift, and it is approaching closing time at 11:00 p.m. You are actually counting down the minutes till you can go home, and you have begun to clean up for the evening. Two people at the register are purchasing desserts to go when we walk in. I step up to the register to ask one simple question: "Do you still have soup?" I wait for the response of the server behind the counter, and it is absolutely perfect.

"Yes, we do have soup."

I reply, "I know how much it sucks when customers come in right before close and order food. Are you sure?"

Her response? "No problem, whatever you would like." Not only is she pleasant, but all three employees working that night are as well.

Kudos to Lisa Boyle and her crew at the Chocolate Cafe in Columbus, Ohio. They truly *get* customer service. What a pleasant customer experience it was for everyone involved. So I ask you this: *What would you do?*

It's important to have an open mind and to deliver

as a customer-service professional. Step up your game every single day, even when you feel it isn't possible. I am telling you that it *is* possible. Reassure yourself frequently, and wake up each morning with the attitude that "today is going to be a great day!"

Become the reason people want to do business with you.

CRUMBS

WAKING UP

Before you even get out of bed, prepare your blueprint for the day. Wrap your mind around the idea that "today is going to be a great day." Get yourself into a routine of positive affirmations. You might want to meditate to get your body, mind, and soul balanced. Use your creative side and write positive messages in a journal, or use the journal to unload your emotions if necessary. Leave your emotional baggage at home so that you can focus on the needs of your customers.

I know you're getting hungry for more customer-service inspiration, so let's look at some preliminary customer-service issues to warm up before viewing the menu. Are you ready to stretch your mind?

You will need to begin with a self-assessment on four key elements in preparing yourself for a customer: demeanor, body language, attitude, and mood. These are their definitions (from *Merriam-Webster*):

Demeanor: a person's appearance and behavior; the way someone seems to be to other people

Body language: movements or positions of the body that express a person's thoughts or feelings

Attitude: a settled way of thinking or feeling about someone or something, typically one that is reflected in a person's behavior

Mood: a conscious state of mind or predominant emotion; feeling; also, the expression of mood especially in art or literature

With an understanding of these four components, you're more likely to have positive interactions with your customers. Take a moment to assess where you are on a scale from one to ten (one being poor and ten being excellent) as you rate *your* demeanor, body language, attitude, and mood using the self-assessment on the next page. Look in a mirror if you must, because positioning yourself properly to be customer ready is of utter importance. What you are trying to achieve in the end is a positive customer experience. Your intention matters. This should eventually become second nature because it's all about being present at the exact moment you need to be. If you are unable to score in the range of eight to ten on each of these questions, then you will need to modify whatever it is you scored low on. Get yourself together. You are in control of you.

Change can happen when you step out of your own way.

Self-Assessment

Demeanor

- Is the way I present myself inviting?

- Is my behavior appropriate?

- Am I approachable?

Body language

- Is the way I position my physical being conducive to interaction with a customer?

Attitude

- Do I have a positive attitude today?

Mood

- How is my mood today—am I happy, upbeat, fun, crabby, irritated, frustrated, or mad?

As Rachel Ray has coined the term *EVOO* (extra-virgin olive oil) on her cooking show, I will coin the term *DBAM* (demeanor, body language, attitude, mood) for customer service in this book. This is a reminder right now to check your DBAM before we start to chow down on the menu items. Let's take this journey together, starting now with the appetizers. Are you with me?

Enjoy the menu. Let your palate take you through an assortment of dishes that will enhance your attitude with every customer you serve. I now present the menu to you.

If you treat your customer like a transaction you will make little progress. If you treat customers with respect, you will see magic happen before you.

THE MENU—ATTITUDE

APPETIZERS

Acknowledgment

A crisp bed of smiles topped off with a friendly "hello"

Initiation

A warm demeanor with a side of inviting body language and conversation

Engagement

A large platter of pleasant interactions

ENTRÉES

Knowledge

An elegant plate of intellect topped off with confidence

Passion

A bowl of caramelized emotions served with a drizzle of intense flavors

DESSERT

Care

Rich, heartfelt concern with a special sauce of hope

Doesn't the menu look great? Did you see anything you would order? If I were a customer, I would order one of each. My hope is that you would too.

Do not underestimate your strengths. They are the gateway to your success.

Just hold on for a minute. I don't really mean to tease you. I must bring up one important but very touchy subject before continuing, one that revs people up, especially in this day and age. Here's the question: *Is the customer always right?* There, I just asked you one of the most challenging questions you will probably ever be asked in your customer-service career. My answer might surprise you, and it is *yes*. OK, I said it, so hear me out on this one.

Ultimately, the goal of any business is to make the customers' experience so remarkable that they will return. There is a positive or negative rippling effect, depending on the outcome of each customer's experience. *Rippling* means one person relays his or her experience to ten people, who in turn tell ten more people, and so on. It gets better than that now, thanks to social media. So multiply those numbers by, let's say, ten, one hundred, one thousand. And it doesn't stop there. I don't have to tell you how powerful social media is, because you see it every day—Facebook, Twitter, LinkedIn, Instagram, and much more. A bad experience can spread like wildfire. Think about your own experiences when you have told your family and friends about how horrible or fantastic an experience was for you as a customer at an establishment.

It's time to change your mind-set regarding the customer always being "right" and think about the ramifications of the answer versus its literal meaning.

So, how well you handle any issues that arise sets the tone for the entire experience. As a customer service community, we need to put the barriers down, think about the end results, and make sound decisions.

It costs less to please a customer who stands before you than to bring in the cleanup crew later on down the road.

When asked, "Is the customer always right?" your response should be yes. Always work your tail off to ensure you've done everything possible to help your customer and to make it a good experience. Of course situations arise that are less favorable in changing a dissatisfied customer's perspective. Stay positive, and talk it through with your customer. Find a middle ground, and compromise. Sometimes that's all it takes for the customer to feel good about the end result. Each of us has the ability to compromise. We all have an internal meter that can be swayed more than we might be willing to admit, so don't be too fast to react, and instead attempt to steer a negative situation in a positive direction.

Say a customer approaches you with a product she purchased and wants to return. In the beginning of the conversation, you might think the customer wants all of her money back, when it turns out all she really wants is store credit. Don't automatically assume the worst in all situations. Your customer, by asking for store credit, just showed you she loves your store and wants to continue shopping there. Listen, and learn. Sometimes the only thing a customer wants is for you to validate her frustration. Validation can be so simple, and yet it's so hard for many. In two words—*I understand.*

Customer dissatisfaction can stem from a variety of issues. So, how do you feel about a guarantee on a product or services—a money-back guarantee? If you stand by your product and are passionate about what you offer, you should have no problem extending a guarantee. "What do I gain from that?" you might ask. You gain customer trust, which translates to repeat customers and referrals. And the same is true of the customer being right.

There is no reason to argue with a customer and get all tangled up in the fact that "the customer is wrong," even if the customer *is* wrong. What you are aiming for in the end is a satisfied customer. It might seem like you are losing a battle, and you might not even reap instant gratification from tending to your customer, but down the road you are *always* a winner. When you remove yourself emotionally from a situation and make a conscious decision not to react to a customer's complaints, it will be beneficial to you and your well-being. Remain neutral, and if all fails rise above confrontation. You will feel emotionally centered and proud of yourself for doing so.

In fact, let's think about this more with the following scenario. I want you to be the customer for a moment. You have a doctor's appointment for your foot. You had surgery two weeks ago, and it's time to get your stitches out. Boy, are you excited! You sign in at the front desk, the receptionist greets you, and you wait to be acknowledged. She asks you for your name one more time and looks at you as though she has just seen a ghost.

Guess what? Your name is not on the schedule. The receptionist asks you what time you thought your appointment was scheduled for. "Two o'clock," you reply, with a tone that reflects that you are a bit frustrated. The receptionist is now getting frustrated because you're raising your voice. She looks at the schedule one more time, and she realizes your appointment is scheduled for 2:00 p.m. the following day.

"Oh sure," she mumbles under her breath. You hear what she says, and the situation escalates out of control.

Do you see how this works? Is the customer wrong? Sure, in this case, but there is a lesson to be learned here. Now let's change this up a bit. You check in for your appointment, and the receptionist sees that you are not on the schedule. She tells you to have a seat and calmly takes control of the situation. Realizing that your appointment is scheduled for the following day, she figures out a way to add you in so you don't have to reschedule. Once again the customer is at fault, but the receptionist takes the initiative to handle the situation. Does the receptionist need to make a big deal about the appointment? No, she doesn't. Instead she removes her emotions from the situation and takes care of the issue at hand. After all, this incident is not about the receptionist. It is about a customer making an honest mistake.

Check your emotions when you feel yourself getting all wrapped up in conflict. What is important to remember here as a customer-service professional is to do the best you can to remedy the situation. Do the right thing by keeping your attitude in line with what you want to accomplish as a customer-service professional and, just as important, as a company.

I bet you are starving at this point. The appetizer is a great place to start. First and foremost, you are going to want to check your DBAM. *Now, are you ready?*

Customer service can be as easy as treating the customer the way you would like to be treated. That should be your default button.

444

CRUMBS

APPETIZERS

~Acknowledgment~

A crisp bed of smiles topped off with a friendly "hello"

Are you the first person customers encounter when they arrive at the establishment where you work? Acknowledging a person who is standing right in front of you—or, in some cases, on the other end of a phone call—might seem elementary, but some customer-service professionals tend to fall short on this in so many ways. Have you ever been a customer yourself and stood at a counter, just waiting for someone to acknowledge your presence? Remember a situation when you were put on hold for an extensive amount of time. How did that work for you? It wasn't so pleasant, was it? Your goal is to see to it that this never happens to one of your customers.

Don't forget that just as a customer's attitude can be detected in many ways, so can yours—tone and body language are two examples. Standing with your hands on your hips will not help your cause, and neither will responding to a customer with an ugly or condescending tone. The interesting thing about attitude is that some people don't think they have an unsavory one until it is pointed out. It is vital that you know the importance of acknowledging a customer or client.

You will never get a second chance to make a first impression.

—Will Rogers

Read the above quote again. First impressions are significant and will mark the beginning of your interaction with customers when acknowledging them. Although first impressions can be very subjective, do your absolute best to make yours count. Just focus on your DBAM to reduce any possibility of misunderstanding. Your attitude at this very moment sets the tone for the rest of the experience. All customers should be treated equally. Don't let the way people look affect the way you acknowledge them as customers. You are doing yourself a disservice as a professional if you dare to go there.

Do you remember the movie *Pretty Woman*? There is a scene where Vivian, played by Julia Roberts, walks into an exclusive shop to buy some clothes. Her appearance falls short of the stereotypical sophisticated boutique shopper. The sales associate snubs her, and Vivian ends up leaving the store very discouraged. The next day, Vivian returns to the exclusive shopping district with Edward, played by Richard Gere. After a whirlwind shopping experience and with her arms full of shopping bags, she returns to the boutique where she was snubbed to tell the associate she made a horrible mistake, especially because she worked on commission.

As many times as we hear the saying "don't judge a book by its cover," we all fall short at times by doing the exact opposite. There is always a lesson to be learned regarding the impressions we make on others.

Don't look now, but a human being is standing in front of you.

The moment the customer presents him- or herself to you, be attentive and on top of your game. The first look you give, or first word you speak, matters to your customer. Embrace the fact that the individual in front of you chose to be your customer. There is no better way to show your gratitude than to acknowledge and greet the customer properly.

Have you ever had an experience that triggered something in you enough for you to stop, think, and take action to try to make a difference? I have, and it's the reason why I decided to write this book. My sister and I encountered an unpleasant customer-service experience while at a spa resort for a long weekend. Soon after I was diagnosed with multiple sclerosis, my sister invited me to join her for a spa weekend. I immediately jumped at the opportunity, and we excitedly made plans. My sister was living in Chicago, and I lived in Dublin, Ohio, so we picked a destination central to both of us. Besides, she had been reading about this particular resort and had been wanting to go for a while. We both work hard as health-care professionals and were excited to get away for some relaxation. In fact, we were so excited about this trip that we arrived at the resort at the exact same time. The odds of that happening are staggering.

We brought our bicycles, and we were eager to try anything over the course of the weekend. The resort has two beautiful hotels on its grounds. The very first day, we rode our bikes from our hotel to the other and walked in to inquire about the spa. We were greeted by an attendant who, in my opinion, clearly did not want to be there. Yes, we did have on T-shirts and shorts. Maybe we looked a little too casual, but that shouldn't have mattered, should it? Our intention was to spend the entire day at the spa, so we asked for a tour to see what it had to offer. Instead of the tour we requested, we were directed to look through a window behind the attendant for a viewing of the pool. Dumbfounded, we peeked through the window, said thank you, walked out, looked at each other, and just shook our heads. The attendant didn't seem interested in selling any packages whatsoever—a far cry from being warm and welcoming.

We got back on our bikes and trekked back to the hotel where we had been staying. Thinking we would get a better welcome at our hotel spa, we walked in to inquire about openings for massages. We stepped up to the counter, and the sales associate barely turned to look at us. We said hello, and the conversation started eye-rolling from the attendant when my sister asked if there were any appointments available for massages. It actually appeared to me that we were putting her out; therefore, my first impression of her went quickly down the tubes.

She responded (with an attitude), "Do you want a male or female massage therapist?"

I replied, "I would like a female."

My sister replied, "It doesn't matter to me; either one is just fine."

The attendant replied, "We don't have hardly any appointments available for females if at all, and only a couple for males."

I was starting to feel a little uncomfortable at this point.

My sister replied, "OK, how about the sugar scrub?"

Her response was, "By the way, the mineral water puts off an odor—I just want you to know that before you schedule anything."

I was thinking, "Oh boy, this isn't going well." It felt like she was trying to deter us from scheduling any services at the spa. Her attitude was so out of line that the other attendant working behind the counter on the computer piped in and said, "Oh, the sugar scrub is great—it leaves your skin feeling so soft."

The conversation went nowhere, and the attendant's attitude turned everything sour, leaving a bad taste in my mouth. I turned to my sister and said, "I'm OK with not going to the spa."

As you read this story, did you think about how you would have acknowledged our presence at the spas? It would have been nice to hear something along these lines at the first spa: "I would love to take you on a tour of our spa. Give me one moment, and I will be right with you."

And at the second: "Welcome to our spa. How can I help you today? Here's our brochure and what we have to offer. I'll give you some time to look it over. I would love to answer any questions you may have about our services."

Not only did the attendants from the two spas share their negative energy with us, the tone and body language they used weren't so great either. Had they offered us two free days at the spa, I would have said, "No, thank you."

If you learn only one thing from this book, let it be that every single person who comes across your path has a story. As a customer-service professional, know that the customer might be there for a reason beyond anything you can fathom. Now, you tell me how important it is to acknowledge your customer in a positive light and with an upbeat attitude. You have the power to ruin a significant day in the customer's life, but you are also equipped to make someone's day better than you imagined as well. Let me give you some tools to help you accomplish this. There are three basic things to remember:

1. Be professional.

2. Make direct eye contact with your customer.

3. Communicate in a manner in which your DBAM reflects your willingness to help your customer.

Start out by extending a greeting in a pleasant voice, making direct eye contact with your customer. For example, say, "Good afternoon, Ms. Smith, welcome to our establishment. How can I help you?" If she is a repeat customer, you will earn extra brownie points if you remember her name—a personal touch. Do you have any idea how someone feels when you remember his or her name? *Special* is the one word that comes to mind. There are a lot of tricks to remembering an individual's name. Listen, and then repeat it as often as possible. Write it down. When I forget a person's name, I go through the alphabet in my head until it comes to me. However, you need to develop your own way of remembering. What works for one person might not work for another.

In acknowledging your customer, you are attempting to build a relationship. If you are busy helping another customer, excuse yourself for a moment from the present customer and quickly communicate to the new customer that you will be with him or her momentarily.

At this point you have just had a taste of the first appetizer by acknowledging the customer. It is time to move forward and engage even more with the customer. "Initiation" just happens to be the next menu item. Before you move on, reflect for a while on what you just read. Be honest with yourself when answering the following questions:

- Am I confident working in the customer service industry?

- Am I approachable?

- Do I acknowledge the customer respectfully and in a welcoming manner?

Before moving on to the next menu item, I would like to mention something about DBAM again. Although we frequently need to assess where we are in the DBAM realm of customer service, it is worth mentioning that it is nearly impossible to be "on" 24-7.

Nothing can be more frustrating than having a bad day, but everyone has one from time to time. It's how we handle the bad day that propels us to a new level. I would say I wake up 99.8 percent of the time in a great mood. I am definitely a morning person. I will tell you some interesting information. If I go to work on an off day, I am quickly reminded by my coworkers that I'm not my usual self. I tend to wear the 0.2 percent of unpleasantness on my sleeve once in a blue moon. As a matter of fact, my crabby self can change the mood in the room instantly. I'm called on the carpet without hesitation. I have such great coworkers who will do that for me. Funny, right? So what are some things you can do if you're having an off day?

1. Admit it.

2. Meditate.

3. Take the day off to recharge.

4. Reflect (journal).

5. Talk it out with someone close to you.

6. Exercise.

> *A positive attitude causes a chain reaction of positive thoughts, events, and outcomes. It is a catalyst, and it sparks extraordinary results.*
>
> *—Wade Boggs*

CRUMBS

~Initiation~

A warm demeanor with a side of inviting body language and conversation

I have worked in the service industry for over thirty years in one capacity or another. In my opinion, initiating conversation is one of the most important interactions you have with your customer. This is when it becomes real. Your customer can sense how genuine you are and how much you care about her or him as a person.

Walk with me into this gift shop while I tell you a story. Great, let's go. We open the door to a boutique-like gift shop and casually walk in. There are many unique items displayed on the shelves. As we approach the back of the store, the associate greets us and notices I am wearing a shirt that reads *Got Pierogi?* To initiate conversation, he blurts out, "You are in trouble for wearing that shirt." I look at him and laugh, and he continues. "My best friend and I used to cook together. Your shirt brings back memories." We have further conversation about family and friends and cooking—we've connected. I walk out of the store smiling.

To this day, I clearly remember that experience. Positive human interaction is extremely crucial to good customer service. It would have been easy for that sales associate to stand silently, but he didn't. He chose to initiate conversation with me. He welcomed me into the store. Because of his comment regarding my shirt, I venture to say that he evaluated my presence as I walked in. He started a conversation that was appropriate for the circumstances, and he seemed to be very genuine.

Restaurants get a bum rap sometimes, so I want to add another feel-good story here. One evening after visiting a friend in the hospital who had given birth to her second child, my family and I decided that going out for dinner would be a great idea. We voted on which restaurant we wanted to go to, and we ended up at Monte Carlo Italian Kitchen in Westerville, Ohio. We pulled up and parked our car, but we weren't quite sure if the restaurant was still open. I took a closer look at a sign hanging on the window; the restaurant closed at 9:00 p.m. It was 8:50 p.m., and guess what? We walked in the front door. There was a woman cleaning in the front dining area. "Are you still open?" I asked.

She replied, "Sure, we are still open."

We smiled and proceeded to follow her to a table. The entire place was empty except for the staff, who were apparently performing their closing duties before leaving for the evening. Kudos to you, Kellie and Dan Ison, for welcoming us with open arms into your restaurant ten minutes before close. The entire experience was enjoyable, from our server initiating pleasant conversation with us to a great dinner. I appreciate your hospitality, Kellie.

Remember, your DBAM should always remain the same, regardless of circumstances. If and when the customer speaks, be present.

Let's take time to review the "appetizer" of initiation:

1. Be professional.

2. Be genuine.

3. Listen to your customer.

Now that's a mouthful, and I have faith that you can do it. It is time to put your fork down and digest all of this thought-provoking food. It's Crumbs time.

- Are you generally outgoing or shy?

- How do you feel about initiating conversation with a customer?

- Can you initiate conversation with a customer without false pretense?

Don't look now, but a human being is standing in front of you.

CRUMBS

~Engagement~

A large platter of pleasant interactions

This is a big appetizer. Your conversation with the customer is moving to the next level. Whereas some customers enjoy engaging in more conversation, others want to get right down to business. There is nothing small about engagement. So at this point, it's time to remind you to continue to gauge your DBAM. It's imperative for you to understand that if any change occurs in your DBAM, you can almost count on it affecting how you engage with your customer.

I will let you in on one of my biggest pet peeves. I'm at a restaurant with my family, and the server decides it is OK to sit in the booth, or in an empty chair at the table, to take our order. *Umm...no!* Can I say that and be politically correct? Well, I'm saying it. Respect your customers' space. Everyone has boundaries. If you don't personally know your customer, be careful not to cross that line.

There are instances in customer service when you have repeat customers, and one of the reasons for that is not only because you are providing good products and services, but also because you build good rapport with customers. You have earned your own base of customers, and they *want* to do business with you. This is referred to as *relationship building*. You might be more playful with regular customers because you are familiar with them, but respect and professionalism are always at the forefront of all interactions.

What happens if a customer walks in and is immediately confrontational with you? It is to your advantage *not* to go down the road of being confrontational in return. Fuel feeds fire. Stay true to who you are and what you are trying to achieve. Engage in a way that will be helpful to your customer. You may just want to sit and listen. When you put water on a fire, it is likely to go out. Now put a dab of fuel on that fire and see what happens. It's best to put the fuel away. I want you to think about what I mentioned earlier in the book: everyone has a story. The irritated customer might have just had a fender bender or received bad news. Has that given you a new perspective on why a customer might act a certain way? It should.

It's not socially helpful or emotionally healthy to take others' behavior personally. In my opinion, 99 percent of the time, it is not about us but about the situation, as I mentioned early on in this book. The other 1 percent is about how someone else perceives our attitude. We are so eager to react, and when we react in a negative fashion, the result is less than favorable. Instead we should put the defense mechanisms away and just listen—a valuable lesson for our personal lives as well.

Now that you are settling in with your customers, they are consciously or subconsciously evaluating how you treat them. In the end, the customer's total experience matters. Continue to work your magic. Whether it's small talk or in-depth conversation, engaging with customers allows them to feel that they're in the right spot. Get comfortable with talking, and let your authentic personality shine— but watch for signs that enough is enough, because everyone has a saturation point. Let me remind you, though, that if you want a loyal customer base, engage and be the difference between competitors.

Do you have a pet? I had two dogs and one cat. Why am I telling you this? Well, after putting two of my pets to rest in two years, the unimaginable happened. Annie, my dog, was noticeably sick. She had a blue tongue and panted uncontrollably one night shortly after coming back from a family vacation. After a little research and watching how she was acting, I knew in my heart of hearts how sick she truly was. I took the day off and called my veterinarian's office as soon as it opened. I was given an appointment to bring Annie in immediately. The minute I walked through the door, carrying her in my arms, I started to cry. Annie's groomer, whom she loved, was standing at the desk and said, "What are you doing here? I had a cancellation this morning, and I was going to call you." Annie had a grooming appointment scheduled for the following Monday. Seeing what state I was in, the groomer quickly escorted us to an exam room and began to pet Annie and console me.

The door to the exam room opened, and it wasn't our usual veterinarian standing there. I was a bit anxious, to say the least. She introduced herself to me and examined Annie as she asked questions about what had been going on with my dog. At one point in our conversation, she asked me if I had ever met her before because I looked so familiar. Honestly, she could have been my longtime neighbor, but at that time my answer would have been the same—no. My mind was only on Annie. This is when the doctor's engagement with me became very real. She asked to take Annie to the back for some tests, which I agreed to. After some time, the doctor came back into the room holding Annie and handed her to me.

"I remembered where I have met you before," she said. "You helped me so much one day where you work. You were so kind." And then she hugged me.

The results from the testing were not good. That morning I made one of the toughest decisions I had to make in a long time, which was to put Annie to sleep. Holding her the entire time, I knew she was at peace because she didn't have to struggle to breathe any more. Before I left the veterinarian's office, the doctor approached me again and said, "You made the right decision. It is exactly what I would have done for my dog." This was something she couldn't have told me before, to avoid swaying any decision I was to make for Annie. What ended up being one of the longest days was also one of the most memorable for me. I will never forget what the doctor said that morning. The doctor took time to engage in conversation with me when she really didn't have to say much at all. Instead, she made a decision to put herself out there and engage with me. This is an ultimate example of engagement and real person-to-person interaction.

I don't know if there is any great place to start the next conversation, but because this part of the menu is all about engagement, it's most likely to get in your way right here. I'm referring to technology. Technology can get in the way of your job performance. Overuse of cell phones and tablets prohibits us from meaningful connections with one another. There is definitely a place and time for electronics, and it isn't when you have a customer in front of you. In-person communication skills, which enable us to have great conversations with people, are deteriorating.

It is frustrating, to say the least, to walk up to a counter for help and see that the clerk, receptionist, or other customer-service professional is texting on his or her phone. I repeatedly see this in many different facets of industry, from high-end hotels to doctors' offices to retail outlets. As a society, we must learn to find balance between staying technologically connected and engaging in face-to-face interactions. The difficult part is this: our lives have become very busy. We communicate with our children, families, and friends using this technology. We also conduct day-to-day business with the same technology (our cell phones, tablets, and laptops). The word I would like to bring into this conversation is *discreet*. Making a noble attempt to be discreet when needing to use your electronics will help you to focus on the task at hand and your customer.

It's time to review the "appetizer" of engagement:

1. Be professional.

2. Be yourself.

3. Focus on the task at hand.

The greatest discovery of all time is that a person can change his future by merely changing his attitude.

—Oprah Winfrey

There are many different opportunities to engage with your customers. This is your chance to ask yourself the following questions and think about changes that you may need to make along the way. Grab a pen and write your thoughts down on the following Crumbs page.

- Do you find it difficult to talk to people?

- Do you think you are a good listener?

- What could you do to become a better conversationalist?

Teressa Shivers-Mazzei

CRUMBS

ENTRÉES

~Knowledge~

An elegant plate of intellect topped off with confidence

We are now at the meat-and-potatoes part of the menu as we venture into the first entrée. If you love what you're selling or the service you're providing, you are knowledgeable about it. The excitement in your voice is telling, and you burst at the seams to help the next customer. It is more than pleasing when a salesperson tells you exactly why the sugar scrub you are interested in is good for your skin as her eyes light up with genuine excitement. It is incredibly helpful and satisfying when a clerk provides detailed specifications regarding a machine part your company needs to order. Although millions of dollars are spent on knowledge, you can't put a price tag on it.

Knowledge + Pride + Confidence = Return Business

The number-one rule when it comes to knowledge is that if a customer asks a question about something you don't know, find the answer. Be honest; tell the customer that you don't know the answer to the question, but you'll be happy to research it. The customer will respect you for your honesty. When you commit to helping a customer, it is of utmost importance to follow through on that commitment. Have you ever heard the saying "Underpromise and overdeliver"? This is when you have to put yourself in a position to make a promise to a customer. As far as I am concerned, you should always try to do the best you can in all capacities of your job, including following through with your customer. What if you changed your thought process to "overpromise and overdeliver"? It's a strategy that might make you appear to be a star, but shooting for authentic, star-quality customer service makes you *feel* like a champion.

How does this all tie in with your attitude? A positive attitude offers a willingness to learn and improve. Here is a simple example. Have you ever been to a restaurant and asked the server the specials of the day? The server rattles the specials off in a descriptive manner that makes you want to order every single dish. On the flip side, there are servers who, when asked the specials of the day, respond with a blank expression. *Bam!* There you have it. When you take time to educate your customers, you have their attention. You are building a level of trust, which is priceless.

Be a sponge, learning as much as you can regarding the tools of your trade, and your reward is confidence. Your ultimate goal is to know your product inside and out, so you can sell it to anyone. Strive to be the best at what you do.

Let's review the first "entrée" of knowledge:

1. Strive to learn.

2. Be proud of what you do.

3. Have confidence in yourself.

Don't accept mediocre. Make the best out of every day. Charge forward to make it spectacular.

A huge part of learning is having the will to do so. Now you are truly thinking like you want to make a difference. Have the courage to grow and learn by pondering the following questions, and take time to write your thoughts on the Crumbs page that follows.

- Are you knowledgeable about the product or service you represent for your company?

- Do you believe in it and take pride in the product or service you stand behind?

- What steps will you take to truly be knowledgeable as a customer-service professional?

Teressa Shivers-Mazzei

CRUMBS

~Passion~

A bowl of caramelized emotions served with a drizzle of intense flavors

Sometimes it takes years before people know what they're passionate about, and that's OK. There are people who will go through their entire lives not knowing, and that is OK too. This is my point: Find something you truly like to do and go with it. Going to work every day will be a lot more enjoyable. I don't care if you're working in a restaurant, a bowling alley, or a doctor's office. Your niche is out there. All you have to do is find it and then do it well. If you like working with people, customer service may be a perfect home for you, and I am glad you are here right now. Unless you work with a machine and a machine only, customer service will be part of your job; it is all around us. Share your passion with your customers through your treatment toward them.

Customers can tell if you are passionate about your job when they meet you. Passion comes from within, and it shines throughout your entire being. You catch their attention—in fact, you outright surprise them—with your enthusiasm. When I talk about customer service, I can't help but get excited. Customer service has been my life's work. When first out of college, I worked at a Hallmark store, then in the restaurant industry, owned my own business, and presently serve in the medical field—over thirty years in customer service. I love working with people. The smile on a customer's face or a warm thank-you over the phone is what I strive for on a daily basis.

Reflect on your own experiences as a customer. I will say this multiple times: treat people the way you want to be treated. Don't you feel good when you go into a store to buy something and the clerk helping you is excited about her job? The last time I purchased a cell phone, I wasn't sure what I wanted. The sales representative had one of the phones I was interested in. He took time to educate me about the phone and to answer any questions I had regarding the phone. He swayed my decision to buy the same phone he had because of his enthusiasm. It sounds almost ridiculous, doesn't it? Passion is contagious. I could probably sell you a pen if I was passionate enough about it. In fact, if I get outright excited about a product or service, you better believe I will tell you about it. And by the time I am done telling you about my experience, I have sold you on it.

Do you ever go to a restaurant and you're not sure what to order, so you ask the server which of two menu items is better? I do that all the time. Imagine that the server passionately describes her favorite dish and tells you she eats it for lunch every other day, describing it in a way that grabs your attention from the get-go. You find yourself ordering it, right? That's the power of passion. The customer-service professional has some credibility. Being passionate about what you are selling is the key to unlocking the door.

Think about all the jobs you have had and what makes you tick. Being happy at work is important, right? Whether a part-time job, transition job, or full-time job, find something you are passionate about. A level of passion is vital to your career success.

If you do not like your job, ask yourself what it is you would prefer to do. Ask yourself, *Am I being true to myself and those I work with and for?* Do some soul-searching, and find your passions. Meanwhile, if you are stuck in a job you do not like, show dignity; work to the best of your ability until something else becomes available. It will pay off in on-the-job experience, along with good references and skills to include on your résumé. We have all been there from time to time and know that every position you hold is a stepping-stone to the next.

It's time to review the "entrée" of passion:

1. Love what you do.

2. Show your enthusiasm.

3. Be proud.

No matter what you do and how big or small your job is, passion and pride play big roles in how you treat people and how they perceive you. Be passionate about your job, and your passion will show through. It is a sense of pride that echoes throughout your work.

It's Crumbs time. What are you passionate about, anyway? It's a really hard question, I know. This may take you some time, but you need to start somewhere.

- What are the things you love to do in regard to customer service? Make a list.

- What are the things you do not enjoy doing in regard to customer service? Make a list.

- What are the ways in which you can demonstrate that you love what you do?

CRUMBS

DESSERT

~Care~

Rich, heartfelt concern with a special sauce of hope

But wait, there is more. Saving the best for last—dessert! Is this all starting to make sense to you now? You have to treat people the way you want to be treated. This is one of my mother's favorite sayings. It's time to do a quick table turn again. Ask yourself how *you* like to be treated. There is absolutely no room for attitude at dessert time. This is when people smile. The end is when the look of fulfillment glows on your customer's face. If you are a dessert person, like I am, you know what I am talking about. The end is about comfort. There are few things more comforting than eating a wonderful dessert, especially when the person who made the dessert cared about the end result. This is what you are striving for. Your task is to care about the outcome of the customer's experience, and this is simpler to do than many people realize.

I am going to take you on a journey to Disney World. If you haven't ever had an opportunity to experience "the happiest place on earth," you should. Disney World parks pride themselves on customer service. I am a true believer after an unbelievable experience at the park. It was spring break 2014 when our family headed to Disney World. I remember this particular day as if it happened yesterday. We decided not to stay at the

Disney resort to save some money—our first
mistake. Even so, we made the best of it. There
were various days that we had arranged for a
character breakfast, tea, or dinner.

On this very day, it was breakfast at the Floridian
Hotel, first thing in the morning. We woke up,
jumped into the rental car, and headed to the hotel
for some fun and food. Everything was prearranged,
so we pulled into the lot, stopped at the gate to
announce our arrival for breakfast, and pulled up to
the most beautiful hotel. Everything works like
clockwork at Disney, as is expected. We had the
most pleasant breakfast. The staff was awesome,
and so were the characters. After breakfast we left
our car in the hotel lot and hopped on a Disney bus
that took us to one of the parks. We had a blast at
the Hollywood theme park that day and arrived
back at the Floridian Hotel late in the evening after
watching the show Fantasia (a must-see) at the park.

We were all dragging, and this is where it gets
good—our second mistake. When it was time to get
the car keys out and head back to our hotel, they
were gone. We all looked at one another with blank
stares. What, no keys? I could barely feel my legs at
this point. It was around midnight. So we walked
into the Floridian Hotel to rehash the day's events
to anyone who would listen. An attendant at the
hotel had told us that the lost and found was closed
for the night and reopened at 9:00 a.m. sharp. By
the way, there is only one main lost and found for

all of the Disney parks. All lost items are taken to one location. Is that amazing or what?

We were anxiety ridden at this point, but this is when a whole lot of wonderful happened. The gentleman helping us at the service counter at the Floridian Hotel called a cab for us, and the hotel paid for it. Yep, that really happened. Here is the clincher—I mentioned this early on, but it is worth repeating: we weren't even guests at the resort, and the Floridian Hotel paid for our cab. The next morning, we called the lost-and-found office and learned that someone had found our keys at one of the gift shops and handed them in. We blamed the entire mishap on Walter, a Muppet that was purchased at the gift store. We still talk about this experience and probably will for a long time to come. Someone showed us that he cared about our well-being, and it was the employee at the Floridian Hotel. He saw that we were at our wits' end and took care of us. Where do you think we are going to stay next time we go to Disney World? You guessed it! We are going to stay at the Disney resort in one of the Disney hotels. I now know that spending the extra money is well worth it and that I am going to be taken care of.

Reflecting on our customer-service menu, up to this point you have done everything right. All it takes is a couple of comforting words to ensure you did all you could for the customer. For example, you might say, "Mrs. Smith, I am so glad you chose our resort. I hope you had a wonderful stay. We look forward to see you in the future."

Focus on genuine and simple conversation. Another example is, "Thank you for your purchase. I hope you enjoy it. We appreciate you and your business." People spend their hard-earned money on products and services every day, so show your appreciation that they chose your business.

Last but not least, let's review the "dessert" of caring:

1. Treat people with respect.

2. Show your customer you care.

3. Don't forget to thank your customer.

As you practice the principles on the customer-service menu, you will find that they are helpful tools of the service trade. Although its basis remains the same, the menu is an ever-changing work in progress as your day-to-day interactions with people unfold.

If you are a person who understands the process, then you are very valuable to your chosen profession.

Final thoughts for your Crumbs page:

- Do you care what your customer thinks?

- Do you think you care enough to make changes in your DBAM?

- How can you improve as a customer-service professional after reading the menu?

The true connection between you and your customer happens when you care.

CRUMBS

CHECK, PLEASE

I'm so excited to conclude with this great story. It reminds me that there are kind people wherever you may go. My sister and I were walking through a set of doors at a resort pool, and two people were approaching us. We held the door open for the couple, and in passing we acknowledged them by saying, "Have a great day."

The gentleman replied, "You have a better one."

I loved his response. I now say that to customers when ending a phone conversation. The customer's typical response in return is great. I can practically hear the individual on the other end of the phone smile.

Use kind, positive words as a daily practice. Your attitude reflects who you are, and it carries over to all aspects of your life. Customer service can be as easy or as hard as you make it. Love what you do, take care of your customers, and at the end of the day, ponder these questions:

- How important do you think your attitude is in relation to what you do?

- How has this book changed the way you think about customer service?

- Name three things you will change about your DBAM tomorrow that will improve your customer-service skill.

CRUMBS

THE HUDDLE

Consider each of the following five scenarios. Drawing upon the concepts and ideas that have been presented in the menu of customer service, use the Crumbs page to list three ways you can use your DBAM to facilitate the outcome of each event so that the customer leaves with a positive perception.

1. You work as a communication specialist answering phones for a doctor's office. A patient calls the office; before you can ask her for her name, she starts yelling into the phone.

2. You are at work, and your phone rings. You are expecting a phone call from your daughter's school, and there are two customers standing in front of you at your register.

3. You are the owner of a very busy bakery in town. You sell cakes and cookies as well as other miscellaneous specialty items. A customer walks in with a cake he had purchased and would like a refund.

4. It is a very busy afternoon at the oil-change and tire shop where you work. Technicians have just completed work on a customer's car. The customer walks up to the counter to pay for her service. You give her the total, and she looks at you with a puzzled

expression on her face and hesitates in pulling her wallet out.

5. You work at a registration desk at a hotel, which can be very challenging. The hotel has multiple conferences scheduled throughout the entire week. An upset customer calls the front desk to express her dissatisfaction with the location of her room. She explains that she had made her reservation three months prior to the conference she is attending at the hotel and specifically asked for a room overlooking the Las Vegas strip. The hotel is sold out, and no such rooms are available.

6. This is your second shift at the restaurant where you work. Two servers called in sick today, and you were asked if you could stay and work a double. You agreed, and now you are approaching one of the tables in the section belonging to the server you replaced. The customers are upset because they have been waiting for over fifteen minutes without an acknowledgment.

Make today a better day because of what you learned yesterday.

Teressa Shivers-Mazzei

CRUMBS

APPENDIX

EMPLOYER DEBRIEFING

Attention employers, managers and supervisors: this section is for you. Although many of you are very familiar with this entire process, it is important for me to reiterate a couple of key points. The basics of customer service start with DBAM. Hiring people who can work with the menu will be extremely important to your success. There is a lot you can teach your employees, and although you cannot necessarily make them have a great attitude, you can be a terrific influence by remaining upbeat and positive. Just as you expect your employees to treat customers well, it is imperative that you, as an employer, manager or supervisor, treat employees the way *you* would want to be treated. So maybe it's time for you to take a deep look at your DBAM. A good attitude can be a powerful morale booster that runs through your business like a happy dance. Once one person gets the positive-attitude itch, it spreads. Hire for attitude, passion and a hunger to learn. This is your opportunity to mold and mentor an eager employee. It might take you a little bit longer to train less skilled individuals, but if they enjoy the job, it may be the difference between profit and loss in the end.

Focus on helping your customer-service team work at the top of its game. Training is the best tool you can give employees; it will set them up for success within your organization. It sounds so cliché, but it's true. Education enables employees to have the confidence to carry out the necessary tasks and fulfill the duties associated with their jobs. Empower your employees so that they can make great decisions and be confident in doing so.

Be a great teacher and an awesome example. Learn from the experts in your field. Attend conferences, network, and read books and articles to find ways to keep your team motivated. Attitude is correlated with the energy of those around you. Work should be a place where your employees thrive. Work is where your employees come together in a cohesive manner to reach goals as a team and to blossom as individuals. Attitude plays a big role in assuring that all of this will happen. Attitude is a benchmark for success.

Appreciation for those on your team is a notably great way to show them they are doing a wonderful job. There is no better way to show your employees appreciation than in the form of a reward. Now let's talk about how you are going to reward your employees for upholding high standards as set forth by you and or your corporation. Yes, *reward them*. If you want to keep good employees, you need to take care of them. Loyalty goes both ways. It costs your business between 16 percent and 20 percent of an employee's annual salary to replace those who make $30,000 to $50,000 a year. The price for loyalty is reward. Reward comes in various sizes, shapes, and forms. A monetary reward is, no doubt, pretty high on the wish list when it comes to rewarding an employee, but believe it or not, verbal recognition rates high, too. Taking time to tell an employee you appreciate all of his or her hard work pays off big time. If people just felt appreciated at work, there would be a noticeable increase in production. Imagine an entire organization feeling appreciated. What do you think would happen to employees' DBAM then?

Last, show your employees that you care. Take time to listen to them. There is something to be said for feeling like you matter. Your employees are putting their hearts and souls into their work for your bottom line. They spend more time with you than they do with their own families. Actions speak louder than words, so please consider the following:

- Be a great role model.

- Educate your employees.

- Empower your employees.

- Appreciate your employees.

- Show your employees you care.

CRUMBS

ACKNOWLEDGMENTS

There are many people I would like to thank for their support along the way. To Carrie, Roberta, Susan, Jessica, Geri, Amy, Melodie, Ann, Shelley, Patti, Gina, and Pam, you pushed me to be better and helped by reading, editing, and planting seeds in my head so this book would become a reality. To my colleagues, thank you for putting up with the many conversations regarding this book—it is finally here. Always remember, your attitude demonstrates the true essence of what being positive is all about. Finally, I extend thanks to my family members, who never stop loving me. I am grateful and thankful for all that I have and all that I am, and I am excited about the journey ahead.

There is no better day to be yourself than today. Show your beautiful colors to all who cross your path.

ABOUT THE AUTHOR

Teressa Shivers-Mazzei has always been passionate about customer service, and she loves interacting with people. She holds a bachelor's degree in recreation leadership and management along with an associate's degree and a leadership award in culinary arts. She has worked in the customer service field for over thirty years and was the owner-operator of a small business, buckeyes on-a-stick from 2006–2013. Teressa has spent the last nineteen years working in the medical field where she has had experience managing team members as well as having daily contact with patients. It is her vision to make a difference, and to bring old-fashioned customer service back to the forefront.

She lives in Ohio with her partner and daughter.

The best way to find yourself is to lose yourself in the service of others.

—Gandi

It is time to get your DBAM on!